DEVELOPMENT WITHOUT DAMAGE
Food and Water

Rob Bowden

A$^+$
Smart Apple Media

Contents

Introduction

If you live in Europe or North America, it is likely that you take your food and water for granted. In other parts of the world, however, there are millions of people who struggle every day to find enough food and water to survive. Solving this problem is an urgent priority, but it also presents some serious challenges. Water and food are not readily available everywhere, and even if they were, not everyone would have access to the amounts that are consumed in more economically developed countries (MEDCs). There are simply not enough resources for everyone to use them at that level.

In MEDCs, more than enough food is available for the population, and in some countries, people suffer from health problems caused by eating too much.

A Global Problem

Food and water are considered to be basic human rights, which means that everyone should have enough of both to survive. Despite this, an estimated 840 million people were suffering from hunger in 2006, and up to 1.5 billion lived without enough water. These figures refer to having just enough to survive. If the amount of food and water consumed by someone living in France or the United States was used as a measure of how much people should have, then these numbers would be even higher. This raises an important question about how much food and water we actually need. Many people in MEDCs now suffer health problems because they eat too much. Waste is another big issue. Vast quantities of food and water are wasted every day—food and water that could be helping to meet the needs of others.

Changing Trends

Long ago, people tended to grow just enough food to feed themselves and their families, and to trade within their communities. As societies developed and people traveled farther, trade in food expanded and diets changed. In MEDCs in particular, there was a move toward more meat-based diets, rather than traditional, largely vegetarian ones. The amount of meat being eaten has increased by more than 500 percent in the past 50 years, and there are now more chickens on Earth than there are humans to eat them!

In recent years, processed foods have also become popular in MEDCs. The problem with these changing trends in diets is that making processed and meat-based food involves a lot more water, energy, and other resources than traditional or vegetarian diets.

Another change has come about because of improvements in transportation and food technology such as refrigeration, packaging, and preservation. In wealthier nations, it is possible to buy strawberries in the middle of winter, fresh tomatoes all year round, and exotic fruits that could never be grown in the countries that import them. The demand for such items in MEDCs can place a strain on resources in other parts of the world—resources that include the water needed for growing and processing food.

All these issues have made governments, organizations, and individuals think carefully about how food and water resources are used and distributed around the world. Providing a growing global population with enough food and

EXPERT VIEW

"Each calorie of meat takes far more water to produce than a calorie of grain, so one of the simplest ways to increase the ratio of food produced to water consumed is to reduce dependence upon meat."
COMPASSION IN WORLD FARMING, *REDUCING MEAT CONSUMPTION: THE CASE FOR URGENT REFORM*

water to keep them healthy, without damaging the environment or using up more resources than necessary, is a big challenge. However, there are a number of ways of developing the food industry more sustainably to help make sure there is enough for all.

Around the world, billions of people do not have easy access to a water supply for drinking, washing, or growing crops, and many have to travel long distances to collect water.

Feeding the World

In 2005, the population of the world passed 6.5 billion. By 2025, it is expected to reach eight billion. This rapidly growing population has placed ever-greater demands on supplies of food and water. The impact on the world's resources has been enormous. Forests and wetlands have disappeared, lakes and rivers have been drained, seas and oceans overfished, and grasslands pushed to their limits—all to provide more food and water.

Predicting Disaster

In the late 1960s and early 1970s, scientists began to predict a global food crisis that would threaten the lives of hundreds of millions of people. They suggested this would be caused by a rapidly growing population and a shortage of resources to feed them. Although the world population nearly doubled between 1965 and 2005, the predicted global crisis never happened on the scale scientists expected. Instead, developments in food and water technology helped crops to grow, turned deserts into farms, and prevented disaster on a massive scale.

In the early years of the twenty-first century, scientists once again began talking about a food and water crisis. The growing population is still blamed as a factor, but there are other reasons now, including climate change, poor farming methods, and a world trading system that many people think is unfair to several countries. In early 2008, there were food-price riots in a number of countries, including Bangladesh, Egypt, and Haiti, and some people think riots like these are signs of this emerging disaster. But what is the real evidence for a twenty-first century crisis, and what is being done to solve the problem in a sustainable way?

Students in Haiti, in the Caribbean, riot in protest against rising food prices. Around 80 percent of the population in Haiti lives in poverty.

Measurements of Success

Although the rise in the world's population has had a negative impact on the environment and resources (see pages 12–13), the priority to produce more food and water has been largely successful. One way of measuring how successful it has been is to look at global calorie intake—the number of calories (energy from food) that each person receives on average per day. In the early 1960s, this was around 2,280 calories per person per day. By 2007, it had increased to 2,800 calories per person per day. In the same period, the number of people who lived in countries where the calorie intake was usually low had fallen. Today, less than 10 percent of the population lives in countries where the average calorie intake is less than 2,200 per person.

There have also been big improvements in the number of people who have access to enough water, particularly in India and parts of Africa. For example, in India in 1970, only 17 percent of the population had access to a safe water supply. By 2002, that had increased dramatically—to 86 percent of the population.

TAKE ACTION

There are many ways that people can help save water. These include

- Turning off the tap when brushing your teeth.
- Taking a shower instead of a bath.
- Monthly charting the water meter to encourage efficiency.
- Collecting rainwater for watering gardens.
- Only using a washing machine or dishwasher when it is full.
- Washing food in a bowl of water instead of under a running tap.
- Fixing leaky taps to avoid wasting water.
- Fitting a low-flush toilet or putting a water-filled plastic bottle in the toilet cistern to reduce the amount of water used.

CASE STUDY

Ghana: Water Policies

In the 1970s, the people of Ghana in West Africa suffered severely from a lack of safe water supplies, particularly in rural areas. Since that time, the government and a number of international organizations have made efforts to create sustainable policies that will allow many more people access to water. In towns and cities, water facilities such as treatment plants have been modernized and improved. The Oxfam Water for Survival program has worked with a local organization, Rural Aid, to help dig wells and provide pumps for people who live in villages, so they do not have to walk long distances to fetch clean water. In 2008, the National Water Policy was introduced, aiming to further improve the situation in Ghana. Already, 76 percent of the population has access to clean, safe water supplies.

This sewage-treatment plant in Ghana separates solid from liquid waste. The liquid is then purified so it can be safely returned to rivers and used again.

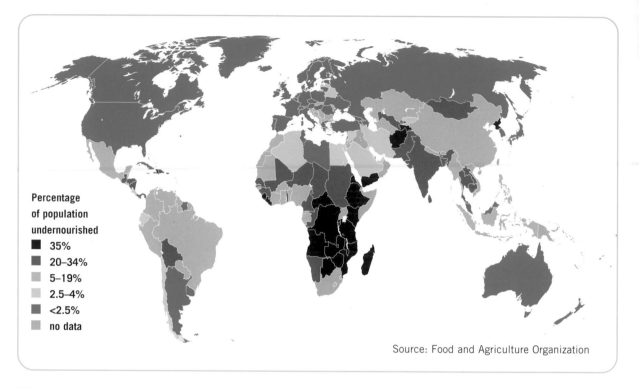

Percentage
of population
undernourished
■ 35%
■ 20–34%
■ 5–19%
■ 2.5–4%
■ <2.5%
■ no data

Source: Food and Agriculture Organization

This map shows the areas of the world suffering most severely from malnutrition.

Still Not Enough . . .

Although many more people now have access
to enough food and water than half a century ago,
the problem has not been solved. Seventeen
percent of the world population—around 1.1
billion people—still do not have access to safe
water supplies, and around one in seven people go
to bed hungry every night. More importantly, the
progress made during the last half-century may be
slowing down. In 2006, the United Nations Food
and Agricultural Organization (FAO) compiled a
report that suggested the number of malnourished
people actually increased from 823 million to 830
million between 1990 and 2004. Most of these
people lived in sub-Saharan Africa. There
is very little rainfall here, so water supplies are
limited and not enough crops can grow. Growth
in world agriculture is also expected to slow down
considerably in the next 40 years—and if there is
less land being farmed, there is less food available.

. . . In the Right Place

In 2008, the number of people in the world
suffering from malnutrition was greater than the
population of all the countries in the European
Union and the United States put together. Although
there is enough food in the world to feed everyone,
the problem is that it is not distributed equally.
The average person living in the United States, for
example, has a calorie intake more than twice that
of someone living in the Democratic Republic of
Congo. But malnourishment is not just about
calories, it is also about the balance and quality of
diet. People who get all their calories from just one
food type are still at risk of malnutrition.

Food Distribution and Diet

It is important to understand the problem of
food distribution because, as the food and farming
industries become more global, the quality of food
is affected as well as the total amount of food
available. For example, a farmer in Kenya might

decide that instead of growing vegetables to feed himself and his family, he will grow them to be exported to supermarkets in MEDCs. This means that he will have to buy food for himself because he is no longer growing it for personal consumption. As many farmers are now exporting their vegetables, they are in short supply in Kenya, and so it is expensive for the farmer to buy them. He may not be able to afford vegetables and will have to buy cheaper food such as corn or beans instead, which do not have the same amount of vitamins and minerals as vegetables. The farmer's diet becomes poorer because of the export trade.

It is clear that providing food for everyone is a complicated issue. Shipping surplus food from one part of the world to another might provide some answers, but it will not meet the need for everyone to have a healthy and balanced diet.

This Somalian boy is suffering from malnutrition. Thousands of people died from the condition during a famine in the country in the 1990s.

FACTS IN FOCUS
Malnutrition

Malnutrition is a medical condition in which people do not have enough nutrients in their diet for their bodies to function properly. People suffering from malnutrition will have very little energy. They are more likely to become ill or catch diseases. Malnutrition can even lead to death. The World Health Organization has stated that malnutrition is a more serious threat to the world's public health than any disease. It affects people of all ages, but children are the largest group suffering from malnutrition, most of them living in Asia and Africa.

EXPERT VIEW

"Malnutrition is estimated to contribute to more than one-third of all child deaths, although it is rarely listed as the direct cause. Lack of access to highly nutritious foods, especially in the present context of rising food prices, is a common cause of malnutrition."
WORLD HEALTH ORGANIZATION

Fishermen sort and pack fish from a trawler. Fish stocks are under threat as the fishing industry expands.

Overfishing

Many experts believe we are approaching a breaking point in food and water supplies. They argue that even if we are able to increase the amount of food being produced, the environment would not be able to cope. An example of this problem is fish stocks. As more and more fish are being caught to provide food for the growing global population, stocks of some fish, including cod and sole, have dropped to dangerously low levels in certain areas. There is a risk that some species will die out, or their numbers will be so much reduced that there is no longer enough to feed people. The reduction in fish stocks is not only caused by overfishing, though. Other factors have also contributed, including pollution, climate change, and "bycatch" (see Facts in Focus).

Laws limiting the numbers of species that can be caught are a step toward reversing the damage to fish stocks, but there are other solutions. Marine reserves can be established—areas where no fishing is allowed at all. One-third of the Great Barrier Reef in Australia is now a marine reserve, for example, and sea life there is increasing. People could also stop buying fish that are under threat.

Soil Erosion

In agriculture, too, there are signs that the environment cannot cope with demand. Crop yields in many areas are declining as soils lose

FACTS IN FOCUS
Bycatch

Bycatch describes marine creatures that are caught by accident by fishing trawlers. Sometimes the fish are the right species, but they are too young and small to be sold. Around half the cod and haddock caught in the North Sea, for example, are thrown back, dead or dying. Some bycatch is fish of the wrong species. The shrimp industry has the worst record—up to 80 percent of the species caught in shrimp nets is bycatch. Bycatch can also include marine mammals like whales and dolphins. They usually die before they can be released back into the sea. Some fishing boats now have special escape hatches that force the whale or dolphin out of the net and back into the sea.

their fertility from being farmed too intensively. Farmers keep up production by applying more and more fertilizer, but this can end up contaminating local water supplies. In countries like Brazil, areas of forest have been cut down to make way for farmland, and natural vegetation has been removed so crops can be grown. These activities have also led to soil erosion.

There are a number of sustainable solutions to the problem of soil erosion. One of the most effective systems is called "crop rotation." Planting the same crop in a particular field every year can reduce the nutrients in the soil, resulting in soil erosion, so many farmers now change the crops they plant in a field each year.

Water for Food Production

Seventy percent of the world's freshwater is used for agriculture, but increased population, polluted supplies, and environmental changes are leading

Contour farming can limit the amounts of freshwater used for irrigation. Fields are plowed along the lines of the slope, which slows down rainwater runoff.

to shortages of freshwater. Shifts in agricultural production, changes to the global trade system (see page 36–37), and improvements in farm technology and water efficiency are all seen as potential solutions to the current challenges.

CASE STUDY

Central Asia: The Aral Sea

The Aral Sea in Central Asia is a dramatic example of what happens when people do not consider the long-term effects of crop production. Large amounts of water for irrigation were diverted from the rivers that ran into the Aral Sea—so much so that by 2007, it was only one-tenth of its original size. Dam projects are now under way to try to reverse the damage and start restoring the sea. Other suggestions have been made, including pumping water from the Caspian Sea into the Aral basin and diverting water from other rivers in the region. These are all expensive solutions, but they could save the sea within two or three decades.

An 8 mile (13 km) long dam has been built to keep in the water that is now returning to the Aral basin.

Biofuels

The growth of biofuels is one of the most recent forms of competition for land and water resources to emerge. Biofuels are fuels that are made from plant-based sources, and they are increasingly being used because they are a more environmentally friendly alternative to fossil fuels.

The majority of the world's transportation depends on oil as a fuel source, but oil is also a big contributor to climate change, because when oil-based products like gasoline and diesel are burned, they release carbon dioxide. Many nations have started to use biofuels instead of oil-based fuels in order to reduce carbon dioxide emissions. The United Kingdom, for example, has set a target for biofuels to make up at least five percent of all fuel sold at pumps by 2010, while the United States has set a target of 15 percent by around 2017. Other countries are making similar commitments, so the demand for biofuels is increasing.

Biofuels and Rising Food Prices

Growing crops that are made into biofuels can provide farmers with a good income, so many farmers are choosing to grow biofuel crops rather than food crops. As more land is given over to biofuel crops, less is available for cultivating food crops. If less food is produced, costs rise. Food prices are increasing all over the world, and many people have blamed biofuels for this. In the European Union, for example, the price of rapeseed oil rose by 63 percent between 2003 and 2007, mainly due to its increased use as a source of biofuel rather than as a food product.

FACTS IN FOCUS
Rising Food Prices

The World Bank said that average food prices in May 2008 were around 2.5 times higher than in 2002. The organization is especially concerned about the impact of these price rises in LEDCs, where up to 80 percent of household income can be spent on food. It has been suggested that up to 100 million people could be plunged back into poverty as a result and that prices are likely to remain high for several years to come.

A bioethanol production plant in the United States. In the United States, 20 percent of the corn grown is used for bioethanol.

their fertility from being farmed too intensively. Farmers keep up production by applying more and more fertilizer, but this can end up contaminating local water supplies. In countries like Brazil, areas of forest have been cut down to make way for farmland, and natural vegetation has been removed so crops can be grown. These activities have also led to soil erosion.

There are a number of sustainable solutions to the problem of soil erosion. One of the most effective systems is called "crop rotation." Planting the same crop in a particular field every year can reduce the nutrients in the soil, resulting in soil erosion, so many farmers now change the crops they plant in a field each year.

Water for Food Production

Seventy percent of the world's freshwater is used for agriculture, but increased population, polluted supplies, and environmental changes are leading

Contour farming can limit the amounts of freshwater used for irrigation. Fields are plowed along the lines of the slope, which slows down rainwater runoff.

to shortages of freshwater. Shifts in agricultural production, changes to the global trade system (see page 36–37), and improvements in farm technology and water efficiency are all seen as potential solutions to the current challenges.

CASE STUDY

Central Asia: The Aral Sea

The Aral Sea in Central Asia is a dramatic example of what happens when people do not consider the long-term effects of crop production. Large amounts of water for irrigation were diverted from the rivers that ran into the Aral Sea—so much so that by 2007, it was only one-tenth of its original size. Dam projects are now under way to try to reverse the damage and start restoring the sea. Other suggestions have been made, including pumping water from the Caspian Sea into the Aral basin and diverting water from other rivers in the region. These are all expensive solutions, but they could save the sea within two or three decades.

An 8 mile (13 km) long dam has been built to keep in the water that is now returning to the Aral basin.

Competing Needs

Meeting basic human needs is not the only pressure on food and water supplies across the world. Water is needed for industry, for domestic use, and for generating electricity in the form of hydroelectric power (HEP). The land available for farming is also needed for growing crops that can generate biofuels, and to house the growing world population. The competition for water and land resources presents a great challenge—which options provide the most sustainable solutions?

Urbanization

Urbanization is the process in which more and more people are moving to towns and cities around the world. In 2007, for the first time in history, more people lived in towns than in the countryside. By 2050, experts predict that more than 70 percent of the population will live in towns. As cities expand to cope with the numbers of people settling in them, more water is needed to support the growing populations, and more land is needed to build places for them to live. Farmland is taken over by building developments. This is called "urban sprawl."

Building work in Beijing, China, encroaches on farmland on the outskirts of the city.

In Malaysia, farmers like this are in short supply because so many people have moved from the countryside to the cities.

EXPERT VIEW

"Small farmers produce much of the developing world's food. Yet they are generally much poorer than the rest of the population in these countries . . . Dealing with poverty and hunger . . . means confronting the problems that small farmers and their families face in their daily struggle for survival."
FOOD AND AGRICULTURE ORGANIZATION, *FARMING SYSTEMS AND POVERTY*

Many cities were built in areas where food production was high and water supplies were good—both good reasons for locating there. As farmland is taken over by developments, food production is pushed onto less fertile or drier land. This reduces the amount and quality of the food produced, and standards of living in the area drop. The competing needs of urbanization and agriculture for both land and water is already a big challenge for governments.

Rural to Urban Migration

Big cities often attract people from rural areas because they offer opportunities for higher incomes and better services, such as education and health care facilities. This movement from villages to towns is called "rural to urban migration." A study by the United Nations predicts that half of all urban population growth up to 2025 will be as a result of rural to urban migration. This could mean up to 1.1 billion

people—almost all of them in less economically developed countries (LEDCs)—leaving the countryside. Without people to work on the farms, less food is being produced. In Malaysia, for example, around 1.8 million acres (730,000 ha) of farmland are not being used or have unharvested crops, because there are not enough people to work the land. How can people be encouraged to stay in the countryside and farm the land if they feel they will earn more money by moving to towns and cities and working in different industries?

One solution is to improve living standards in rural areas and to offer incentives to farmers to stay on the land. This can be difficult in countries where little money is available, but the World Bank has launched the Rural Development Strategy, which invests in programs to help poor people in rural areas.

Biofuels

The growth of biofuels is one of the most recent forms of competition for land and water resources to emerge. Biofuels are fuels that are made from plant-based sources, and they are increasingly being used because they are a more environmentally friendly alternative to fossil fuels.

The majority of the world's transportation depends on oil as a fuel source, but oil is also a big contributor to climate change, because when oil-based products like gasoline and diesel are burned, they release carbon dioxide. Many nations have started to use biofuels instead of oil-based fuels in order to reduce carbon dioxide emissions. The United Kingdom, for example, has set a target for biofuels to make up at least five percent of all fuel sold at pumps by 2010, while the United States has set a target of 15 percent by around 2017. Other countries are making similar commitments, so the demand for biofuels is increasing.

Biofuels and Rising Food Prices

Growing crops that are made into biofuels can provide farmers with a good income, so many farmers are choosing to grow biofuel crops rather than food crops. As more land is given over to biofuel crops, less is available for cultivating food crops. If less food is produced, costs rise. Food prices are increasing all over the world, and many people have blamed biofuels for this. In the European Union, for example, the price of rapeseed oil rose by 63 percent between 2003 and 2007, mainly due to its increased use as a source of biofuel rather than as a food product.

FACTS IN FOCUS
Rising Food Prices

The World Bank said that average food prices in May 2008 were around 2.5 times higher than in 2002. The organization is especially concerned about the impact of these price rises in LEDCs, where up to 80 percent of household income can be spent on food. It has been suggested that up to 100 million people could be plunged back into poverty as a result and that prices are likely to remain high for several years to come.

A bioethanol production plant in the United States. In the United States, 20 percent of the corn grown is used for bioethanol.

CASE STUDY

Brazil: Ethanol Capital of the World

Brazil first began to use sugar-based ethanol fuels in its vehicles in the 1970s, when oil prices across the world were increasing. Not only was bioethanol cheaper, but it also avoided the risk of fluctuating oil prices that were typical of the 1970s and 1980s. Today, bioethanol fuel is available at around 29,000 filling stations in Brazil and costs around one-third less than gasoline. It accounts for about 20 percent of Brazil's transport fuel market, and Brazil even exports it to Sweden and Japan. Brazil has been criticized by environmentalists, who say that as more farmland is used to grow sugar cane to make bioethanol, other farm activities (especially ranching) are pushed farther into Brazil's fragile forest and grassland ecosystems. The Brazilian government denies this and continues to expand bioethanol production.

A worker in Brazil harvests sugar cane that will be used to make bioethanol. As more biofuel crops are grown, areas of rain forest are cut down to provide more land for food crops.

Wider Effects of Biofuel Production

There are also concerns about the indirect effects of biofuel production. In the United States, many farmers who had previously grown soy are now growing corn instead. The corn is used to make bioethanol, a biofuel, and this type of farming is supported by government payments called subsidies. As soy farmers in the United States switch to corn, farmers in Brazil are encouraged to grow more soy for export to the United States and elsewhere. They do this by clearing new land in the Amazon rain forest or by taking over pastures and driving cattle ranching farther into the forest. This has led to what environmentalists are calling an "arc of deforestation" in the Amazon region. Some people believe this is linked to the increased demand for biofuels.

Others, however, say that biofuels are not to blame and that rising costs and the expansion of farmland have more to do with higher incomes and changing diets in countries like China and India, both of which would lead to a greater demand for food. Biofuels are an important factor in planning a sustainable future for our environment, but which should take priority—addressing the environmental concerns of climate change, or ensuring that enough food is being grown to feed our growing population?

A Green Revolution

The "green revolution" is the name given to improvements in agricultural science and technology that have improved food production. In the past, practices such as greater use of irrigation and the development of chemicals that promoted growth and reduced pests have helped avoid hunger on a massive scale. However, more developments are likely to be needed if we are to avoid a future crisis in food production.

Increasing Land Use

One way to increase production is simply to increase areas of farmland and the amount of water used. This has already occurred in many parts of the world, for example, in the Philippines and China. Agricultural land now covers 37.5 percent of the world's land surface. The amount of freshwater being used has also increased, by 325 percent between 1965 and 2005.

The problem with this expansion of farmland is that it has already destroyed enormous areas of natural habitat. This has had a dramatic impact on wildlife. The populations of many animal species have dropped as habitats are lost to make way for farmland. Expansion has also removed the

The increased use of pesticides and chemical fertilizers has improved crop yields.

important environmental services that these habitats provided. When wetlands are drained for agriculture, for example, they are no longer available to store water, to help with flood control, or to provide a place for fish to breed. In the long term, this can affect food production because the quality of the remaining water becomes worse, risks of flooding are higher, and fish stocks are reduced.

Similar problems can occur when forests are cleared to make way for farmland. For example, forests in the Congo River Basin in central Africa play a significant role in the water cycle—the trees store water from rainfall and release it back into the atmosphere through a process called transpiration. Trees recycle between 75 and 95 percent of rainfall in this area. If the forests are removed, this important natural cycle is disrupted.

Improving Efficiency

As more and more natural habitats are destroyed by a range of human activities, the resources available to meet our food and water needs are reduced. To solve this problem, a lot of attention is now focused on how we might use resources more efficiently. Intensive farming already means that a lot more food can be produced in a smaller area, but the challenge is how to continue this without damaging the environment.

FACTS IN FOCUS
The Intensification of Global Food Production

Year	Arable land acres/person (ha/person)	Grain yield pounds/acre (kg/ha)
1965	0.86 (0.35)	1,464 (1,644)
1975	0.72 (0.29)	1,871 (2,101)
1985	0.64 (0.26)	2,428 (2,726)
1995	0.62 (0.25)	2,471 (2,775)
2005	0.54 (0.22)	2,898 (3,254)

Source: World Development Indicators 2008

Rice terraces in the Philippines. The amount of land used for agriculture in the country increased more than 50 percent between 1965 and 2005.

EXPERT VIEW

"Needed for the twenty-first century is a . . . doubly green revolution in agricultural technology. Productivity increases are still vital, but must be combined with environmental protection or restoration, while new technologies must be both affordable by, and geared to the needs of, the poor and undernourished."
FOOD AND AGRICULTURE ORGANIZATION, *WORLD AGRICULTURE: TOWARDS 2015/2030*

Irrigation

Irrigation provides water for crops in areas where there is very little or unpredictable rainfall. The water for irrigation can be diverted from rivers or lakes, captured or harvested in reservoirs, or pumped from groundwater sources. Across the world, the area of irrigated farmland increased from 368 million acres (149 million ha) in 1965 to more than 692 acres (280 million ha) by 2008. Irrigation has played an important role in improving methods of farming, and many experts see it as an essential part of any further improvements.

There are three main types of irrigation: surface irrigation, sprinkler irrigation, and drip irrigation. They have different levels of efficiency based on how much water is wasted in the process.

Surface Irrigation

In surface irrigation, water is allowed to flood the surface of a field. The water normally reaches the field through a channel with a gate in it, but it can also be pumped onto the field. Surface irrigation is the least efficient kind— up to 60 percent of the water is wasted. It simply runs off the ground or sinks in without benefiting plant growth.

Sprinkler Irrigation

In sprinkler irrigation, water is sprayed in the air to simulate rainfall. Up to 30 percent of water is wasted through evaporation from leaves, by overshooting the field, or through overwatering on the ground.

Sprinkler irrigation uses a system of hoses, pipes, and sprinklers to spray water in the air so it falls on the crops like rainfall. Sometimes a pump is needed.

Drip Irrigation

In drip irrigation, small quantities of water are carried in pipes with small holes that allow water to be released close to the crop roots. Only around 10 percent of water is wasted, and overwatering is less likely because water is delivered more directly.

Crop Yields

In general, more efficient irrigation results in more crops. Unfortunately, the most efficient systems are also the most expensive, so they tend to be used for crops that have a high value or for nonfood crops like cut flowers. Improving irrigation systems so more food crops can be grown is important for three key reasons:

- Irrigated farmland is up to three times more productive than land that relies on rainfall. In 2008, irrigated farmland accounted for around 17 percent of the world's cropland, but produced 40 percent of the global harvest.

- Each calorie of food produced requires about 1 quart (1 L) of water. Limited water supplies are reducing the amount of food being produced, so irrigation systems that use less water for the same result will benefit food production.

- Inefficient irrigation can cause salinization— where surplus water evaporates or raises the water table (the level of water underground) to contaminate the soil with mineral salts that are in the water.

In 2008 only around one percent of irrigated land was managed using the most efficient systems, but these reduced water use by at least 60 percent. The FAO has been experimenting with low-cost drip-irrigation systems that use simple filters and a low-pressure system instead of expensive pumps. These have helped farmers in LEDCs to reduce water use or increase the area cultivated for the same amount of water as before.

A farmer plants garlic next to drip-irrigation pipes in northern India. Drip irrigation delivers water directly to plant roots, limiting water waste.

EXPERT VIEW

"Water, mixed with fertilizer, is pumped through the pipes and comes out here, drop by drop, right by the plant's root. With the same amount of water, this system allows us to double or triple the surface cultivated. Even with less rain, it allows you to irrigate. It means that we can be a lot less dependent on the heavens!"

MARIA HELENA SEMEDO, FAO'S REPRESENTATIVE TO NIGER, DESCRIBING THE BENEFITS OF DRIP IRRIGATION

In countries like Afghanistan, new varieties of crops such as wheat that give a higher yield
have dramatically improved food production and helped avoid a crisis in basic food supplies.

Biotechnology

Irrigation provides just one way of increasing food
supplies. Other technologies are available that also
offer the potential for meeting the world's food
needs in a sustainable way. Biotechnology (plant
science) in particular could hold the key to
avoiding a global crisis—but it also raises many
questions. In the 1960s, the green revolution
looked at plant science as a way of increasing
food supplies by creating high-yield varieties
(HYVs) of staple crops such as rice and wheat.
These new varieties allowed countries on the brink
of famine, such as Mexico, India, and Pakistan,
to grow enough food to feed their populations.

The downside to these so-called "miracle crops"
was that they required a whole package of other
technologies to maximize their effect, including
irrigation, fertilizers, and pesticides. All these
factors increased the cost for farmers. Many

could not afford the package and ended up
losing their land to wealthier landlords. A lack
of training also meant that the use of chemicals
was often inaccurate, leading to pollution of the
local environment and particularly water supplies.
Many farmers also failed to wear protective
clothing when working with the chemicals,
which caused them health problems.

Genetically Modified Foods

A new era of biotechnology is now providing
breakthroughs that go far beyond breeding high-
yield varieties and actually look at engineering new
species. Genetic modification (GM) is a process
that allows scientists to identify the individual
genes that make up all life on Earth and artificially
adapt them in plants and animals. Crops can be
genetically modified to improve their resistance to
certain pests, for example, or to require less water

so that they can be grown in semi-arid (dry) regions. Supporters of GM technology believe it may hold the key to avoiding a global food crisis by increasing yields, raising farm incomes, reducing chemical use, and conserving water. They claim GM crops are better for the environment and can even improve human health by processes such as enriching rice with beta-carotene to increase the production of vitamin A. Vitamin A deficiency causes blindness in 500,000 children and up to two million deaths every year.

EXPERT VIEW

"I am in favor of careful use of this technology rather than careless rejection. Equally I am not claiming that the only choice is between adoption of genetically modified crops and mass starvation . . . We should use whatever we have."

MARTIN WOLF, JOURNALIST AND ECONOMICS EDITOR

FACTS IN FOCUS
Top 10 GM Food Producers

Rank		GM Crop Area million acres (million ha)		Total Crop Area million acres (million ha)	
1	USA	135.2	(54.6)	293.1	(118.6)
2	Argentina	44.5	(18.0)	79.8	(32.3)
3	Brazil	28.4	(11.5)	158.6	(64.2)
4	Canada	15.1	(6.1)	66.9	(27.09)
5	India	9.4	(3.8)	493.5	(199.7)
6	China	8.7	(3.5)	435.2	(176.1)
7	Paraguay	4.9	(2.0)	11.1	(4.5)
8	South Africa	3.5	(1.4)	12.5	(5.05)
9	Uruguay	1.0	(0.4)	2.3	(0.95)
10	Philippines	0.5	(0.2)	31.9	(12.9)

Source: Friends of the Earth International, 2008

Some experts believe that GM food will reduce the amount of chemicals used in farming and limit the risk of pollution to water supplies.

The Problems with GM

GM technology is controlled by a handful of very large companies, which can make large profits from selling GM seeds. There is concern that GM crops will not help the millions of small-scale farmers who need to improve their food supplies. Instead it could put them at risk of price rises beyond their control. Another concern with GM is that "playing with nature" could have unknown outcomes if GM varieties contaminate natural varieties or affect the health of wildlife and even humans. These reasons have led several nations to ban GM crops until they are better understood. In many countries, the public is so against the use of GM crops that many supermarkets have adopted labeling programs to prove that foods are GM free.

Perhaps the biggest concern with GM crops, however, is that in many cases, they have not so far improved food supplies as people hoped. Studies of GM soy production in the United States, for example, have shown that harvests of GM soy can be between 6 and 10 percent lower than non-GM soy. Furthermore, they have only been successful in competing with non-GM varieties where larger amounts of chemicals are used. The seed companies producing GM crops argue against this, and several countries are still carrying out experiments with GM varieties, but it seems that we cannot fully rely on them to meet future needs.

EXPERT VIEW

"Who wants to eat a crop that kills pests who try to eat it? It's not natural. No one I know likes the idea."

LI MING FU, FARMER IN XISHUANGBANNA VILLAGE, SOUTHERN YUNNAN PROVINCE, CHINA

Copying Nature

The opposite of GM technology is to work with and copy nature. Our planet's natural environments are extremely diverse and highly productive, and

A farmer harvests genetically modified corn in the United States. The United States is the largest producer of GM crops in the world.

many scientists believe we could learn a great deal more from them. Organic farming is one method that attempts to do this by reducing the use of artificial chemicals and instead using natural fertilizers and pest control (see pages 26–27).

There are also changes in farming practice that copy nature, such as growing trees and food crops together in a practice known as agroforestry or silviculture. Agroforestry has been shown to increase yields and can also provide many environmental benefits, such as blocking harmful winds, reducing soil erosion, and conserving water supplies.

Another lesson from nature is to combine fishing and farming. This has been done very successfully in parts of China by raising fish in paddy fields planted with rice (see page 31). New varieties of staple crops such as corn and rice could also increase yields of cultivated varieties.

Agroforestry involves planting crops among existing forest areas. It prevents soil erosion and deforestation.

CASE STUDY

Bolivia: Agroforestry

Farmers in the Yungas region of Bolivia rely on crops such as citrus fruit, coffee, and cocoa for their livelihoods. Until recently, the slash-and-burn farming technique was used, in which trees were cut down and the remains burned to clear plots for farming. Even when the land was cleared, it could be up to four years before farmers had a harvestable crop. Slash-and-burn causes soil erosion, so after a few years, farmers would have to move on to a new plot, which caused further deforestation.

In the early 2000s, the Yungas Community Alternative Development Fund (YCADF) began working with farmers on agroforestry methods, planting crops alongside trees. Nutrients in the soil are retained so the plot can be farmed for many years. Agroforestry also results in a harvestable crop in the first year of planting. It has provided farmers with a sustainable income, using sustainable methods that do not harm the environment.

Sustainable Solutions

With concerns growing about the environmental impact of some methods of increasing food and water supplies, there is now a major effort to find more sustainable solutions. The challenge is to improve the supply and availability of food and water without damaging the environment or using up resources for future generations. Organic farming is one of the better-known sustainable solutions, but there are others that focus on either food or water—or, better still, on ways of using food and water together in a sustainable way.

Organic Farming

Before the invention of artificial chemicals, food was grown using the nutrients and defenses that were found in nature—a method broadly known as organic farming. In recent years, organic farming has become more popular again, as a way of addressing concerns about levels of food production and other issues, such as the use of chemicals in farming. Farmers, politicians, and consumers have all realized that although chemical farming may be more productive, the damage it causes to the environment and the additional cost in energy and resources such as fossil fuels make it highly unsustainable. Many people see

A mother and her children farm organic crops in Uganda.

FACTS IN FOCUS
Long-Term Benefits of Organic Farming

A 21-year study by Swiss scientists has found that although organic farming may reduce yields by around 20 percent when compared to nonorganic farming, there are other benefits that more than make up for this in the long term. Energy use was between 34 and 53 percent lower on organic farms, and pesticide use was 97 percent lower. In addition, the soil was found to be in better condition, allowing for the more efficient breakdown of nutrients, and it contained more than twice the number of pest-eating spiders and other insects.

Organic food has become very popular in MEDCs, where people can afford to pay higher prices. Local farmers grow their produce and sell it at markets.

organic farming as a sustainable alternative to chemical farming, and it is a fast-growing method of agriculture. Organic methods of farming are regulated internationally by the International Federation of Organic Agriculture Movements.

The Cost of Organic Food

One of the key problems with organic farming is that it requires a lot more time and skill than nonorganic farming, and many of these skills have been lost during the switch to chemical farming. It takes more time to grow organic crops, and the yields are lower, both of which make organic food more expensive to buy. In fact, this additional cost is exaggerated because the true costs of nonorganic produce, such as the environmental damage it causes, are not taken into consideration. Organic food has also become fashionable and is promoted by celebrity chefs and high-profile campaign groups as being better for human health as well as the environment. Like many fashionable items, this means consumers can be charged more because of high demand for the products.

EXPERT VIEW

"Recent research suggests that if all farming was organic, the slight decrease in yields in the northern hemisphere would be more than matched by overall increases elsewhere, leading to a slight increase in total food production . . . Even with the uncertainties, in a world of increasing scarcity of fossil fuels, organic farming provides the only environmentally, or economically, sustainable system of feeding the world."
PETER MELCHETT, SOIL ASSOCIATION, 2008

Organically grown beans being packed in Kenya. These will be shipped around the world, so the environmental cost of transportation must be weighed against the benefits of organic growing methods.

Organic Challenges

Besides the lower productivity and higher costs, organic farming faces other challenges. First, for food to qualify as organic, the land it is produced on must be certified as organic. It can take several years for land that was farmed with chemicals to return to organic status, and in areas where organic land is close to nonorganic land, there is a risk that crops could be contaminated by chemicals used on the nonorganic land.

A second challenge is the supply of organic produce. The fastest-growing demand is in the wealthier markets of Europe and North America, but these countries do not have enough organic land to meet demand, and so they import large quantities of organic food. The energy needed to transport this food, together with the carbon emissions it generates, often outweighs the environmental benefits of growing organic produce in the first place.

A third challenge is that organic farming methods are more labor-intensive. In the United Kingdom, there is evidence that this has been a positive factor and has helped to provide new

farming jobs in an industry where 80 percent of jobs had been lost since the 1960s. Where there is still a rapid movement of workers from rural to urban areas, however, there may not be enough people to meet the increased labor needs of growing food organically.

Pick and Mix

Replacing chemical-based farming with organic farming may help to reduce the pressure on resources and protect the environment, but if it is to play a key role in the future of food production, it must be shown to actively increase the amount of food provided. A solution to this might be combining some of the principles of organic farming with other farming methods in a sort of pick-and-choose system. An example of this is the System of Rice Intensification (SRI), which combines methods of using land, seeds, water, nutrients, and human labor. The SRI method follows many organic principles, such as the use of compost and manure rather than chemicals as fertilizers. The method also minimizes the use of water by keeping the plant roots moist rather than flooding the whole field, as in conventional rice paddies.

SRI rice can use 25 to 50 percent less water than conventional methods—which is extremely important for the millions of people who live in areas short of water and who rely on rice as their staple food. Most important is the increase in yields. Whether using traditional or hybrid varieties of rice, farmers have reported increased yields of 20 to 40 percent when using SRI instead of conventional methods. When combined with a lower environmental impact and reduced use of water, energy, and resources, this makes SRI one of the most significant breakthroughs in sustainable agriculture in recent years. If SRI was used on 49.4 million acres (20 million ha) of land under rice cultivation in India, for example, experts have predicted that India would meet its 2050 target for increased grain production as early as 2012.

EXPERT VIEW

"The System of Rice Intensification improves yields with less water, less seed, and less chemical inputs than most conventional methods of rice cultivation. This means that the returns on inputs are higher, making the method potentially more profitable than most of the traditional methods. SRI is ideal in giving impoverished rural communities the much-needed food and health security, while conserving scarce natural resources, particularly water."

WWF, *MORE RICE WITH LESS WATER*, 2007

As the food crisis worsens in LEDCs such as India, more farmers are turning to SRI to increase yields.

CASE STUDY

Madagascar: Rice Intensification

The System of Rice Intensification began in Madagascar in the 1980s, and its effects are now fully being felt in its country of origin. Over the past five years, Madagascan farmers have reported that using this system has increased their rice yields more than fourfold. This is particularly important in countries like Madagascar, which cannot afford many of the technologies being developed in other parts of the world to help improve their crop output. There are now programs being introduced to expand the use of SRI to more parts of Madagascar, and it has provided a model for several other countries. In total, 28 countries were introducing SRI in 2008, including China, India, and Indonesia—with a combined population of 2.7 billion.

Urban Agriculture

Urbanization (see page 14) places great pressure on food and water resources, but it can also provide opportunities. In many countries, people moving from the countryside to urban areas bring farming skills with them, and it is possible to find small pockets of farming in even the largest cities. This "urban agriculture" makes use of vacant land to grow vegetables or fruit crops; of the city fringes to grow grains; and of backyards to keep a few chickens or a pig, cow, or goat.

Urban agriculture can improve diets and provide a source of income for people who live in cities. However, there is a danger that it can become a health hazard. Pollution from untreated waste, for example, can contaminate the land and water used for urban agriculture. Sometimes too many pesticides are used in urban plots, and the chemicals in the pesticides can get into drinking water supplies. A 2003 study of *palak* (spinach) sold in Delhi, India, found that virtually all of it failed to meet national health guidelines.

Several cities are now recognizing the importance of urban agriculture and introducing planning and monitoring to better support and control it. In the Cuban capital, Havana, there are more than 20,000 small plots covering some 6,845 acres (2,770 ha) that are farmed by Havana's residents. These are vital to local food production and are strictly monitored by the city authorities to ensure they are safe for consumers.

Reusing Water for Farming

Recycling treated waste water for use in irrigation is a sustainable option with enormous potential benefits to both food and water supplies, especially in light of our rapidly urbanizing world. A city with a population of 500,000 and water consumption of 31.7 gallons (120 L) per person a day produces about 12.7 million gallons (48 million L) of

A man works in his urban plot in the Cuban capital, Havana.

CASE STUDY

China: Rice-Fish Farming

In parts of China, farmers have been sustainably raising fish in their rice paddies for many years. It increases yields of both fish and rice, and it reduces the use of chemicals. The fish eat weeds that would otherwise compete with rice for growing space, and their waste provides a natural fertilizer that boosts rice growth. Rice-fish farming also uses water more efficiently by producing rice and fish from the same water. Across China, rice yields increase by around 11 percent when cultivated with fish, and 2.5 acres (1 hectare) of rice paddy can produce between 330 and 990 pounds (150 and 450 kg) of fish a year. There are human benefits too: less need for weeding, improved diet, and an additional source of income from selling fish.

China has more than 3.7 millon acres (1.5 million ha) of land under rice-fish farming, and other countries are now expanding their use of this technique.

wastewater every day. When treated, this wastewater could be used to irrigate around 1,236 acres (500 ha). The nutrients in the waste are almost as valuable as the water itself! The amount of waste from normal sewage could provide all the nitrogen and much of the phosphorus and potassium normally required for agricultural crop production.

This sewage treatment plant separates the waste from water and recycles it. The recycled water can be used to water crops.

Grow Your Own

It is possible for individuals to grow their own food, even where there is not much space. Many food crops can be grown in small containers and even indoors. People with yards could consider using part of their plot to grow their own food. Digging up lawns in favor of food crops could dramatically alter food production—as was proven during the "Victory Gardens" campaign of World War II. By the end of the war in 1945, the United States had some 20 million gardens, producing around 40 percent of the country's vegetables.

With rising oil prices, growing food shortages, and greater concerns about where our food comes from, many people believe growing our own food will become more popular in the future and that gardens may soon be feeding their owners. China, Japan, Argentina, Kenya, and South Africa are among countries similarly promoting urban agriculture as a sustainable solution to urban food needs.

A small rooftop garden in Shanghai. The Chinese government plans to develop 1.1 million square yards (930,000 sq m) of urban rooftop gardens by 2018.

CASE STUDY

Canada: SkyFarm

An ambitious scientist in Toronto, Canada, has made plans to use a system of growing food in nutrient-rich water (rather than soil) called hydroponics to produce a vertical SkyFarm in the middle of a city. This would be a 58-floor building using recycled water to grow enough food in the heart of Toronto to feed 35,000 people every day! The SkyFarm reduces the environmental impact of having to transport food from outside areas into the city, and because it is a method of indoor farming, the success of crops does not depend on unpredictable weather. Other countries, including the United States, are planning more systems of "vertical farming."

The Living Tower is just one of several vertical farms that are being planned for cities in MEDCs.

TAKE ACTION

There are several ways in which individuals can help protect precious food supplies:

- Avoid food waste by only buying what you need and storing food properly.
- Think about buying locally grown food where you are able to, which helps support local producers.
- Try to buy organic food that supports higher standards of environmental care.
- Only buy fish that comes from sustainably managed sources.
- Find out whether you can join a local community garden to grow your own vegetables. If not, use your own garden or even containers and pots.
- Think about your own diet and the amount of calories you consume.
- Buy fair trade food products to guarantee growers a better price.
- Buy food close to its "sell-by" date if you are going to eat it immediately, so that stores do not end up throwing it away.

Carrots and potatoes spill out of a commercial waste dump. The amount of food that is thrown away in MEDCs is a big concern when seen in the context of the global food crisis.

Reducing Waste

Wasting food and water reduces the sustainability of any practice. Reducing the amount of water lost through leaky pipes and collecting as much as possible from rainwater or graywater recycling (reusing water used from washing, for example) would all contribute to greater sustainability. In Sydney, Australia, wastewater is being treated and reprocessed for use in watering gardens and washing cars. This reduces the use of drinking water for such purposes and helps conserve water resources in one of the driest regions of the world.

In the United States, it is estimated that between 25 and 50 percent of all food ends up being thrown away. The UN World Food Program has said that surplus food from the United States could feed every hungry person in Africa. If it had not been produced and sold to MEDCs in the first place, the food itself and the water used in its cultivation may have benefited LEDCs. Of course, some of it is thrown because it spoils. Those who sell the food and those who buy it could reduce the amount that is sold and bought to prevent it becoming unwanted waste in the future.

Trade and Distribution

No matter how productive and sustainable food and water production become, the world still faces the problem of a mismatch between supply and demand. The trade and distribution of both are therefore just as important to consider in striving for development without damage. Food is one of the most widely traded products in the world, so this is far from simple, but there are ways of improving the trade and distribution of food.

The World Food Trade

Trade in food has taken place for thousands of years, but until quite recently, it was on a relatively limited scale. Modern storage and transportation technologies allowed a significant increase in food trade during the second half of the last century, and they far outpaced any increase in food production. Trade in grains, for example, increased by 251 percent between 1961 and 1999, but production increased by only 137 percent. The amount of meat traded increased by 500 percent over the same period compared to a production increase of 222 percent. These patterns are repeated for trade in vegetable oils, milk, and vegetables and fruit.

Globalization

What these figures mean is that food circulates around the world more than ever before, as part of a process known as globalization. The result of this is that there are more people involved in the food supply chain. At one time, food may have passed directly from farmer to consumer through a local farmers' market, but today it is increasingly likely that consumers buy food from a supermarket or other retailer. The retailer, in turn, may buy from a wholesaler, who buys from an importer,

Sheep being loaded onto a ship for export in Australia. The globalization of the food industry has improved the economies of several nations, but it has also had a negative impact for many small farmers.

who buys from a stock agent, who may finally buy from the farmer.

With so many people in the chain, the money paid for the final product has to be split between all those involved. The parties at the end of the chain, such as the supermarkets selling to you, have much greater power than the farmers at the beginning of the chain. Their buying decisions affect the whole chain and determine what prices farmers will finally receive for their produce. In the United States, for example, for every $1 spent on food, only around $0.19 goes to the farmer—the rest is divided among those further down the chain.

EXPERT VIEW

"The distance between producer and consumer has grown ever wider as world trade in food has increased. Food supply chains have become longer and more complicated, and consumers are often unaware of the source of the food they eat, the conditions for the workers who produce the food, and the environmental impact of its production, processing, packaging, and distribution."

THE EARTHSCAN ATLAS OF FOOD

Buyers inspect frozen tuna fish at a wholesaler's in Tokyo, Japan. Wholesalers are one link in a long chain of food-industry contributors.

Changing Prices

Supermarkets and others at the end of the chain work in a competitive environment and want to keep prices as low as possible to attract customers. This creates a downward pressure on the price of food, which means that over time farmers have received less and less for their produce. The cost of major food commodities (wheat, rice, coffee, tea, cocoa, sugar, corn, etc.) fell more or less consistently in the second half of the last century. In 2002–2003, many were trading at lower prices than they had been 20 years before. Since 2003, the price of many commodities has increased because there is a greater demand for them from rapidly developing economies such as India and China. The growing demand for biofuels and the increased amount of processed foods in our diets are also causing food prices to rise.

These increased prices have benefited many large-scale commercial farmers in countries such as Canada, Brazil, Argentina, Australia, and the United States, but for many of the world's poorest people, it has simply meant an increase in the cost of food. By 2008, food prices faced additional pressures as global oil prices hit record highs.

Huge farms in countries like Canada benefit from the worldwide increase in food prices, but small farmers in LEDCs suffer badly from the same phenomenon.

EXPERT VIEW

"We need to attack market failures and change the economic rules of current food production systems. We must eliminate agricultural and fisheries subsidies that support elites in the North . . . and expand fair trade and labeling processes that create incentives and add benefits to producers in the South . . . We must have greater investment . . . to support food production systems that feed the poor and supply local markets."

GONZALO OVIEDO, INTERNATIONAL UNION FOR CONSERVATION OF NATURE, 2008

In an era of a global food markets, this increase is passed on throughout the supply chain, as each part of the chain has to pay more in energy and transportation costs.

Changing the Rules

In June 2008, the United Nations held a conference to discuss the problem of rising food prices and warned of a major crisis unless there was not only an increase in production, but also a change in the way that food is traded. At the moment, trade is dominated by a relatively small number of hugely influential countries. Many of

these are protected by tax systems that pay subsidies to their own farmers, while charging tariffs on food imported from other countries.

Such systems protect local farming, but have a dramatic impact on world trade because they allow farmers to produce food for less than the true market value (because they are being paid a guaranteed subsidy). This increased production lowers world prices and means farmers growing food in countries without subsidies can see their incomes fall. Subsidies can also influence what is grown. Subsidies on biofuel crops have reduced the area used to produce food, for example, and some say this is at least partly to blame for the food shortages and rising prices in 2007–2008.

The subsidies paid to farmers in MEDCs totalled around $300 billion in 2008. The impact of this is more clearly seen when you consider that just one week's worth of these subsidies would meet the cost of providing food aid to all the world's hungry for an entire year. Scrapping the subsidies may help to free up the world food market and give farmers in LEDCs better opportunities to sell their produce.

The United Nations conference in 2008 addressed the problems of rising food prices.

FACTS IN FOCUS
Agricultural Subsidies

Agricultural subsidies are money paid by governments to farmers to supplement their income. Crop yields can vary depending on factors such as weather conditions, so a farmer's income can change dramatically from year to year. Subsidies mean that farmers have a guaranteed income even in years where crop yields are low. Many people argue that subsidies work against the idea of free trade. Often only wealthier countries can afford to pay subsidies, which means that farmers in poorer countries suffer because they cannot produce crops at competitive prices. Do countries have the right to protect their own farmers, or should there be one law that applies to all and keeps prices the same all over the world?

Fair Trade

One response to existing trade patterns is the fair trade movement. This guarantees farmers a minimum price for their produce that is set above the long-term market average. Farmers can earn up to double the market value during times when prices are low, and if prices rise, then farmers are paid at the market rate. The most important aspect of fair trade, however, is that the guaranteed price allows farmers to plan ahead, and they are often paid a share of the money in advance so they can invest properly in their activities. To qualify for fair trade certification, farmers must also show that they are adopting sustainable practices—that they are farming in a way that protects the environment and invests in the local community.

The fair trade movement began in the Netherlands, but it has since spread to many other countries, including Japan, Australia, the United States, and the United Kingdom. Each country has a special labeling method to show which food products have come from fair trade farmers. This allows consumers to choose fair trade products and contribute to a fairer and more sustainable system of food production.

By 2007, the fair trade movement was working in 59 countries with around 600 producer

A farmer and his son pick fair trade coffee beans in Uganda. Worldwide sales of fair trade produce had reached $1.7 billion a year by 2007, with coffee one of the leading fair trade products.

CASE STUDY

Ghana: Fair Cocoa

In Ghana, an elderly cocoa farmer carries a sack of beans from his farm to the cooperative's store, where he knows the scales will be accurate and he will be paid for the full weight of his crop. This story could be repeated time and again around the world, with farming cooperatives buying their own scales. It is one example of how earnings from fair trade sales enable farmers to take more control over their businesses and their lives. The Kuapa Kokoo Co-operative in Ghana has 45,000 cocoa farmers and is one of the best-known success stories. As well as receiving fair prices for their beans, the Kuapa Kokoo farmers own one-third of the UK-based chocolate manufacturer Divine Chocolate Ltd. This means they also benefit from the value added to their beans when they are made into consumer products and sold.

In Ghana, a woman works on a fair trade cocoa plantation. Here, farmers are assured of a fair price for their produce.

organizations and more than 650 traders. It was benefiting around seven million people—farmers, workers, and their families—in LEDCs.

Success of the Movement

The growth of the fair trade movement and its popularity with consumers has encouraged many major food companies to switch to fair trade products. In the United States, Dunkin' Donuts made all its espresso coffee fair trade in 2006, and the UK-based supermarket Sainsbury's opted to switch all its banana sales to fair trade during 2007. Despite these successes, fair trade still makes up a tiny proportion of global food trade and tends to focus on nonstaple items such as chocolate, coffee, tea, honey, juices, and fruit.

FACTS IN FOCUS
Fair Trade and Fairtrade

The term "fair trade" refers to the idea of farmers earning a decent income from the growth and export of their goods. "Fair Trade" refers more specifically to the labeling system controlled by Fairtrade Labeling Organizations International and the organizations that are part of it. The FLO is the body that sets the standards for fair trade and makes sure they are met.

Cattle ranching is a valuable form of farming in countries like Brazil, but beef has one of the highest virtual water costs of any food type.

Virtual Water

An important part of a sustainable future in food and water supplies is what experts call "virtual water." This is the amount of water that it takes to produce the food we eat—for example, in raising cattle, the amount of water it takes to irrigate pastures, to make the cattle feed, and to process the meat. The amount of virtual water in meat is much more than in vegetables, so as increasing numbers of people around the world eat more meat, more water is used up.

When any type of food is traded around the world, so too is the water that was used to produce it. This has led to debate about where food should be grown in the future and whether it is sensible to always grow food locally, as many who promote sustainable food production suggest. If the country where the food is produced suffers from water shortages, it might be more sustainable to save the water used in producing food locally by importing food from a country with better water supplies instead.

Weighing It Up

Growing food or raising livestock in countries with sufficient water supplies could benefit countries where water is scarce—but only if

The Hidden Water in Our Food

Item	Quarts of water per pound (Liters of water per kilo)	
Wheat	573	(1,200)
Rice	1,289	(2,700)
Corn	1,040	(450)
Potatoes	76	(160)
Soybeans	1,098	(2,300)
Beef	7,159	(15,000)
Pork	2,864	(6,000)
Poultry	1,336	(2,800)
Eggs	2,243	(4,700)
Milk	430	(900)
Cheese	2,530	(5,300)

Source: UN Food and Agriculture Organization

TAKE ACTION

- Find out what your school is doing to promote water efficiency and reduce food waste.
- If you can't find the information you need on a food product, then ask the supplier or store.
- Join a campaign group that is promoting better food, farming, and fishing practices.
- Join a charity that campaigns against world hunger or write to your politician about it.
- Find out what your local water company is doing to promote greater water efficiency.

than is really needed. Trade only works if the end consumer is willing to buy, so consumer power can have a major impact on creating a more sustainable world. We all need food and water, and most of us enjoy access to both without too much trouble, but there remain millions who do not. The increasingly connected nature of our lives means that even the small changes we make can—through the power of trade—make a difference to development elsewhere.

What individuals choose to eat and where they go to buy their produce—a local market or a supermarket—may influence the food trade at a global level.

they can afford to buy the imported foods. With rising oil prices and increased food costs, buying in food (and the water it contains) could be too expensive for many countries, especially as those that suffer from a lack of water are also among the poorest in the world.

The idea of "virtual water" has also been questioned by environmentalists, who are concerned about the negative impact of transporting even more food around the world. Weighing up the overall benefits of virtual water is still something scientists and major organizations such as the World Water Council are working on. One of their concerns is that it could make poorer countries too dependent on foreign trade. One way of addressing this issue might be to introduce a form of "fair water trade," like the fair trade movement in food supplies.

Consumer Power

Changing the way we think about food and water is perhaps one of the most effective ways to influence trade and distribution. Understanding where food comes from and how it is produced (including the water used) can help everyone to make informed choices. Only buying what we need to avoid waste, for example, would make sure that retailers and suppliers did not buy more

facts and figures

Population and Food Production (1965–2005)

Year	Population (thousands)	Crop yield pounds/acre	(kg/ha)
1965	3,313,902	1,464	(1,644)
1970	3,675,901	1,637	(1,838)
1975	4,059,564	1,871	(2,101)
1980	4,431,033	2,066	(2,319)
1985	4,823,325	2,428	(2,726)
1990	5,263,923	2,583	(2,900)
1995	5,676,845	2,471	(2,775)
2000	6,076,654	2,737	(3,073)
2005	6,461,659	2,898	(3,254)

Source: World Development Indicators, 2008

Dietary Energy

Country/Region	Kcal consumed/person/day
United States	3,770
United Kingdom	3,440
Russia	3,080
Brazil	3,060
South Africa	2,940
China	2,940
Japan	2,770
Peru	2,570
India	2,440
Thailand	2,410
Kenya	2,150
Democratic Republic of Congo	1,610
World average	2,800

Source: UN FAO, 2007

Coffee Prices

Year	Price (U.S. cents per pound)
1980	213.07
1985	152.10
1990	70.36
1995	162.81
2000	97.68
2005	93.63
2008	127.93

Source: International Coffee Organization, 2008

Food Miles

Food miles is the distance an item of food travels from the farm to the supermarket. This table shows a basket of nine food items purchased in the United States and how many miles each item has traveled.

Item	Origin	Food miles (km)	
Asparagus	Peru	3,503	(5,638)
Pears	Argentina	6,101	(9,818)
Spinach	Spain	3,651	(5,876)
Grapes	Chile	4,970	(7,999)
Potatoes	Israel	6,550	(10,541)
Tomatoes	Saudi Arabia	7,448	(11,987)
Chicken	Thailand	8,305	(13,366)
Brussels Sprouts	Australia	9,760	(15,707)
Carrots	South Africa	6,730	(10,830)

further Resources

Web Sites

Friends of the Earth International
http://www.foei.org/

Greenpeace
http://www.greenpeace.org/

OneWorld.net's Kids Channel
http://tiki.oneworld.net/food/

Organic Kids Club
http://www.organics.org/kids_club

Oxfam International
http://www.oxfam.org/

UN Food and Agricultural Organization
http://www.fao.org/

World Trade Organization
http://www.wto.org/

Books

Baines, John, *Food and Farming* (The Global Village), Black Rabbit Books, 2009

Baines, John, *Food for Life* (Sustainable Futures), Smart Apple Media, 2007

Bellamy, Rufus, *Food for All* (Action for the Environment), Smart Apple Media, 2006

Bowden, Rob, *Earth's Water Crisis* (What If We Do Nothing?), World Almanac Library, 2007

Bowden, Rob, *Food and Farming* (Sustainable World), Kidhaven Press, 2004

Bowden, Rob, *Trade* (The Global Village), Black Rabbit Books, 2009

Farndon, John, *From DNA to GM Wheat: Discovering Genetically Modified Food* (Chain Reactions), Heinemann Library, 2006

Inskipp, Carol, *Conserving Our Fresh Water* (Sustainable Futures), Smart Apple Media, 2007

Kerr, Jim, *Food: Ethical Debates on What We Eat* (Dilemmas in Modern Science), Black Rabbit Books, 2008

Mason, Paul, *Food* (Planet Under Pressure), Heinemann Library, 2006

Morgan, Sally, *Natural Resources* (The Global Village), Black Rabbit Books, 2009

Glossary

agroforestry a method of farming in which trees and crops are grown together. The trees help keep nutrients in the soil and prevent soil erosion, so crops are improved.

arable land land that is suitable for growing crops.

biofuels fuels made from organic material. Biofuels are often made from plant sources, but they can also be created from animal waste. Biogas, bioethanol, and biodiesel are examples of biofuels.

biotechnology the science of modifying plants and animals to have new characteristics for use in food and farming—for example, increasing a plant's immunity to disease.

calorie a unit used to measure how much energy something has. When used in relation to food, its full name is kilocalorie (Kcal).

certification a process in which an official body like a government or organization ensures that an area or industry—such as organic farming—meets particular standards.

climate change a change in global temperatures that can result in extreme weather conditions. Climate change can happen naturally, but human activities are believed to be increasing the rate of this change.

deforestation the process of cutting down trees from an area so that the land can be used for purposes such as farming.

ecosystem a community of living plants, animals, insects, and the environment in which they live.

erosion the wearing away of soil or rocks by natural forces such as wind or water. Soil erosion can also be caused by human activity such as farming.

European Union an organization of 27 European countries. The EU allows freedom of movement of people, goods, services, and money between its member nations.

exports any goods or services that are sold outside the country in which they originate.

famine a period in which there is a severe shortage of food in a particular area.

fossil fuel a fuel made from living material over millions of years. Coal, oil, and natural gas are examples of fossil fuels.

genetic modification (GM) the process of making some food products bigger, better, or more resistant to disease by combining the genes of different species to develop the strongest characteristics.

graywater water that has been used for domestic purposes such as washing, which is then used for other purposes such as watering gardens.

groundwater water that has seeped below the surface of the Earth and often lies between the soil and rock. Groundwater supplies can be pumped to the surface and used for irrigation or drinking water.

human rights the basic rights and freedoms to which all people are considered entitled. These include rights such as freedom of expression, the right to legal protection, and the right to employment. They also include the right to enough food and water to be healthy.

hydroelectricity electricity generated from moving water.

imports any goods or services that originate outside the country in which they are purchased.

irrigation a system of watering dry land by digging ditches or otherwise diverting water sources to help crops grow.

LEDC less economically developed country—one of the poorer countries of the world. LEDCs include all of Africa, Asia (except Japan), Latin America and the Caribbean, and Melanesia, Micronesia, and Polynesia.

MEDC more economically developed country—one of the richer countries of the world. MEDCs include the whole of Europe, North America, Australia, New Zealand, and Japan.

processed food food that has been altered from its natural state, for example, by freezing, drying, or canning, or by the addition of preservatives or colorings.

resource a useful or valuable substance. Food and water are both resources.

rural relating to the countryside.

staple crops such as wheat or corn that provide the basic foodstuff for millions of people.

subsidy a grant of money that is made by a government to either a domestic seller or a buyer to help cover the cost of producing or selling certain goods and services.

surplus a quantity of a product such as a food crop that is larger than needed.

sustainability the use of resources in a way that means the present generation can have what it needs without damaging the supply of resources for future generations.

tariff a tax placed on goods transported from one country to another, or when they are imported. A tariff raises the price of imported goods, making them less competitive with goods that have been produced locally.

United Nations an international organization, established in 1945, which aims to help countries cooperate in matters of international law, economic and social development, and human rights. There are currently 192 member states in the United Nations.

urban relating to built-up areas such as towns and cities.

urbanization the process in which increasing numbers of people are settling in towns and cities. As urbanization takes place, towns and cities grow larger and expand onto previously undeveloped land.

yield the amount of crops that a farmer can produce.

Index

WILLIAM STEIG

ALADDIN PAPERBACKS

New York London Toronto Sydney Singapore

For Charlotte Reine Steiner

First Aladdin Paperbacks edition May 2003

Copyright © 1968 by William Steig
Revised Format Edition, 2000

ALADDIN PAPERBACKS
An imprint of Simon & Schuster
Children's Publishing Division
1230 Avenue of the Americas
New York, NY 10020

Also available in a Simon & Schuster Books for Young Readers hardcover edition.
Designed by Jennifer Reyes
The text of this book was set in Avant Garde Bold ITC.
The illustrations were rendered in watercolors.

Manufactured in China
2 4 6 8 10 9 7 5 3 1

The Library of Congress has cataloged the hardcover edition as follows:
Steig, William, 1907-
CDB! / by William Steig.
p. cm.
Summary: Letters and numbers are used to create the sounds of words and simple sentences
4 u 2 figure out with the aid of illustrations.
ISBN 0-689-83160-9 (hc.)
1. Word games—Juvenile literature. [1. Word games. 2. Games.] I. Title. II. Title: CDB!
GV1507.W8S75 2000 793.734—dc21 99-32720

ISBN 0-689-85706-3 (Aladdin pbk.)

C D B!

D B S A B-Z B.
O, S N-D!

I N-V U.

R U C-P?

S, I M.

I M 2.

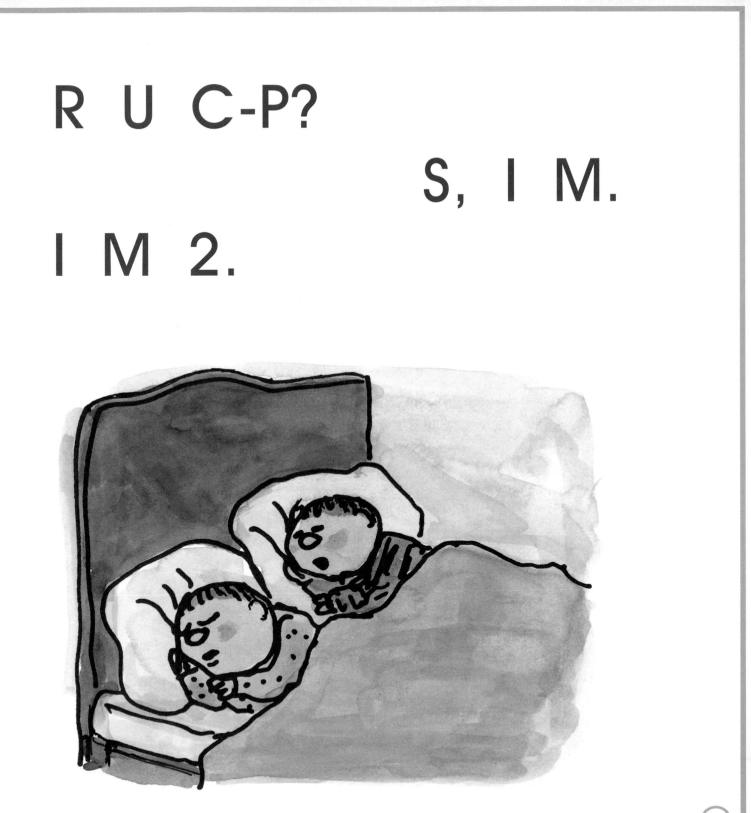

A P-N-E 4 U.

K-T S
X-M-N-N
D N-6.

D N S 5 X.

I M 2 O-L 4 U.

O U Q-T.
U R A B-U-T.

I M B-4 U.

R U O-K?

S, N Q.

I M A U-M B-N.

U R N N-M-L.

D C-L S N D C.

D D-R S N D I-V.

D L-F-N 8 D A.

S E-Z 4 U. S?

B-4 U X-M-N L-C, X-M-N R-V.

H-U!

I C U.

S N-E-1 N?

L-X-&-R N I
R N D C-T.

I N O.

K-T S D-Z.

I C Y.

F U R B-Z,
I-L 1 O-A.

E S D 1 4 U 2 C.

I M N D L-F-8-R.

M N X R L-T 4 U!

I M C-N A G-P-C.

N-R-E S N T-S.

I M N
A T-P.

P-T N J R N J-L.

O 4 A 2-L.

E-R S A M-R.

S M-T!

I F-N
N-E
N-R-G.

I M C-N U!

N-D U R. U R P-K-N.

P-T S N N-M-E.

I O U 6 X.

O, I C M. N Q.

D Y-N S X-L-N!

O-L H.

IOUAJ.

I M N N-D-N.

O, I C.

U 8 L D X!

L-C S N X-T-C.

Answer Key

Page 3	C D B! = See the bee! D B S A B-Z B. = The bee is a busy bee. 0, S N-D! = Oh, yes indeed!
Page 4	I N-V U. = I envy you.
Page 5	R U C-P? = Are you sleepy? S, I M. = Yes, I am. I M 2. = I am too.
Page 6	A P-N-E 4 U. = A peony for you.
Page 7	K-T S X-M-N-N D N-6. = Katy is examining the insects.
Page 8	D N S 5 X. = The hen has five eggs.
Page 9	I M 2 O-L 4 U. = I am too old for you.
Page 10	O U Q-T. = Oh you cutie. U R A B-U-T. = You are a beauty.
Page 11	I M B-4 U. = I am before you.
Page 12	R U O-K? = Are you ok? S, N Q. = Yes, thank you.
Page 13	I M A U-M B-N. = I am a human being. U R N N-M-L. = You are an animal.
Page 14	D C-L S N D C. = The seal is in the sea.
Page 15	D D-R S N D I-V. = The deer is in the ivy.
Page 16	D L-F-N 8 D A. = The elephant ate the hay.
Page 17	S E-Z 4 U. S? = It's easy for you. Yes?
Page 18	B-4 U X-M-N L-C, = Before you examine Elsie, X-M-N R-V. = examine Harvey.
Page 19	H-U! = Achoo!
Page 20	Y R U Y-N-N? = Why are you whinin'? I N O. = I don't know.
Page 21	I C U. = I see you.
Page 22	S N-E-1 N? = Is anyone in?
Page 23	L-X-&-R N I R N D C-T. = Alexander and I are in the city.
Page 24	I N O. = I don't know.
Page 25	K-T S D-Z. = Katy is dizzy. I C Y. = I see why.
Page 26	I 8 U! = I hate you! I 8 U 2!= I hate you too!
Page 27	F U R B-Z, = If you are busy, I-L 1 O-A. = I'll run away.
Page 29	E S D 1 4 U 2 C. = He is the one for you to see.
Page 30	I M N D L-F-8-R. = I am in the elevator.
Page 31	M N X R L-T 4 U! = Ham and eggs are healthy for you!
Page 32	I M C-N A G-P-C. = I am seeing a gypsy.
Page 33	N-R-E S N T-S. = Henry is in tears.
Page 34	I M N A T-P. = I am in a teepee.
Page 35	P-T N J R N J-L. = Petey and Jay are in jail.
Page 36	O 4 A 2-L. = Oh, for a tool. E-R S A M-R. = Here is a hammer.
Page 37	S M-T! = It's empty!
Page 38	I F-N N-E N-R-G. = I haven't any energy.
Page 39	I M C-N U! = I am seeing you! N-D U R. U R P-K-N. = Indeed you are. You are peeking.
Page 40	P-T S N N-M-E. = Petey has an enemy.
Page 41	I O U 6 X. = I owe you six eggs. O, I C M. N Q. = Oh, I see them. Thank you.
Page 42	D Y-N S X-L-N! = The wine is excellent!
Page 43	O-L H. = Old age.
Page 44	I O U A J. = I owe you a jay.
Page 45	I M N N-D-N. = I am an Indian. O, I C. = Oh, I see.
Page 46	U 8 L D X! = You ate all the eggs!
Page 47	L-C S N X-T-C. = Elsie is in ecstasy.